HAMPSHIRE
Wit & Humour

JANE BUF

BRADWELL
BOOKS

Published by Bradwell Books

9 Orgreave Close Sheffield S13 9NP

Email: books@bradwellbooks.co.uk

Compiled by Jane Burberry

British Library Cataloguing in Publication Data: a catalogue record for
this book is available from the British Library.

1st Edition

ISBN: 9781909914575

Print: Gomer Press, Llandysul, Ceredigion SA44 4JL

Design by: jenksdesign@yahoo.co.uk/07506 471162

Illustrations: ©Tim O'Brien 2014

A teacher at a school in Twford was having a little trouble getting her Year 11 pupils to understand grammar. "These are what we call the pronouns," she said, "We use them with verbs like this: I am, you are, he/she is." The pupils looked at her with glazed expressions.

Trying a different tack, she said, "Lauren, give me a sentence with the pronoun, 'I' in it."

Lauren began, "I is..."

"No, no, no, no, no NO, NO!" shouted the teacher, "Never, 'I is', always, 'I am'... now try again."

Lauren looked puzzled and a little hurt, thought a while then began again more quietly, "I... am...the ninth letter of the alphabet."

Simon was down on his luck so he thought he would try getting a few odd jobs by calling at the posh houses in Brockenhurst. After a few "no ways", a guy in one of the big houses thought he would give him a break and says, "The porch needs painting so I'll give you £50 to paint it for me."

"You're life-saver, mister," says Simon, "I'll get started right away!"

Time passes until…

"There you go, I'm all done with the painting."

"Well, here's your £50," says the homeowner, handing over some crisp tenners.

"Thanks very much," says Simon, pocketing the money, "Oh and by the way, it's a Ferrari, not a Porsche!"

Insurance Assessor: "What gear were you in at the moment of the impact?"

Woman Driver: "Gucci sweats and Reeboks."

Two aerials meet on a roof, fall in love, get married. The ceremony was rubbish - but the reception was brilliant.

Two rival cricketers from Petersfield and Waterlooville were having a chat.

"The local team wants me to play for them very badly," said the man from Waterlooville."

"Well," said his friend, "You're just the man for the job."

Portsmouth beat Swindon Town five - nothing; they were lucky to get nothing.

A rather cocky young man, who worked on a busy construction site in Portsmouth, was bragging that he could outdo anyone in a feat of strength. He made a special case of making fun of Morris, one of the more senior workmen. After several minutes, Morris had had enough.

"Why don't you put your money where your mouth is?" he said. "I'll bet a week's wages that I can haul something in a wheelbarrow over to that outbuilding that you won't be able to wheel back again."

"You're on, mate," the cocky young man replied. "It's a bet! Let's see what you got."

Morris reached out and grabbed the wheelbarrow by the handles. Then, nodding to the young man, he said, "All right. Get in."

A couple from the Isle of Wight had been courting for nearly twenty years. One day as they sat on a seat in the park, the woman plucked up the courage to ask,

"Don't you think it's time we got married?"

Her sweetheart answered,

"Yes, but who'd have us?"

One day, a man and his son arrived at the rugby ground to watch the game between Fareham Heathens and Eastleigh R.F.C. But the man suddenly realised that he couldn't find their tickets for the game. He said to his son, "Nip home, Ben, and see if I left the tickets there." "No probs, Dad," answered the boy.

Half an hour later, Ben returned to his dad, who was patiently waiting outside the stadium. "You were right, dad," said Ben, "They're on the kitchen table where you left them."

A lawyer from Salisbury and a businessman from Southampton ended up sitting next to each other on a long-haul flight.

The lawyer started thinking that he could have some fun at the man from Southampton's expense and asked him if he'd like to play a fun game. The businessman was tired and just wanted to relax. He politely declined the offer and tried to sleep. The lawyer persisted, explaining, "I ask you a question, and if you don't know the answer, you pay me just £5; you ask me one, and if I don't know the answer, I will pay you £500."

This got the businessman a little more interested and he finally agreed to play the game.

The lawyer asked the first question, "What's the distance from the Earth to the moon?"

The man from Southampton said nothing, but reached into his pocket, pulled out a five-pound note and handed it to the lawyer.

Now, it was his turn to ask a question. He asked the lawyer, "What goes up a hill with three legs, and comes down with four?"

The lawyer scratched his head. He looked the question up on his laptop and searched the web. He sent emails to his most well-read friends. He used the air-phone to call his colleagues in Salisbury, but he still came up with nothing. After over an hour of searching, he finally gave up.

He woke up the businessman and handed him £500. The man pocketed the cash smugly and dozed off again.

The lawyer was wild with curiosity and wanted to know the answer. He shook the businessman awake. "Well? What goes up a hill with three legs and comes down with four?" he demanded.

The businessman reached into his pocket, handed the lawyer £5 and went straight back to sleep.

Two elderly ladies were enjoying a small sherry in their local in Bramshott.

One said to the other, "Was it love at first sight when you met your late husband?"

"No, I don't think so," came the reply, "I didn't know how much money he had when I first met him!"

A man from Gosport said to his wife, "Get your coat on love. I'm off to the club".

His wife said, "That's nice. You haven't taken me out for years".

He said, "You're not coming with me...I'm turning the heating off when I go out".

A bloke from Winchester goes into an artist's studio and asks if the artist could paint a picture of him surrounded by beautiful, scantily clad women. The artist agrees but he is intrigued by this strange request. He asks his new client why he wants such a picture painted and the bloke says, "Well, if I die before me missus when she finds this painting she'll wonder which one I spent all me money on!"

The next day the bloke's wife goes into the artist's studio and asks him to paint her wearing a big diamond necklace and matching earrings.

"Of course, madam," says the artist, "but may I ask why?"

"Well," replies the woman, "if I die before me husband I want his new woman to be frantic searching for all me jewellery!"

Derek and Duncan were long-time neighbours in Ringwood. Every time, Derek saw Duncan coming round to his house, his heart sank. This was because he knew that, as always, Duncan would be visiting him in order to borrow something and he was fed up with it.

"I'm not going to let Duncan get away with it this time," he said quietly to his wife, "Watch what I'm about to do."

"Hi there, I wondered if you were thinking about using your hedge trimmer this afternoon?" asked Duncan.

"Oh, I'm very sorry," said Derek, trying to look apologetic, "but I'm actually going to be using it all afternoon."

"In that case," replied Duncan with a big grin, "You won't be using your golf clubs, will you? Mind if I borrow them?"

A lad from Bramshaw who had just started his first term at Marlborough College asked a prefect, "Can you tell me where the library's at?"

The older student said disdainfully, "At Marlborough, we never end a sentence with a preposition."

The new boy tried again, "Can you tell me where the library's at, you wally?"

Why was the computer so tired when it got home?

Because it had a hard drive!

Light travels faster than sound. That's why some people appear bright until you hear them speak.

A well-known academic from Salisbury was giving a lecture on the philosophy of language at Southampton University. He came to a curious aspect of English grammar.

"You will note," said the somewhat stuffy scholar, "That in the English language, two negatives can mean a positive, but it is never the case that two positives can mean a negative."

To which someone at the back responded, "Yeah, yeah."

A Hampshire man is driving through Wiltshire, when he passes a farmer standing in the middle of a huge field. He pulls the car over and watches the farmer standing stock-still, doing absolutely nothing. Intrigued, the man walks over to the farmer and asks him, "Excuse me sir, but what are you doing?"

The farmer replies, "I'm trying to win a Nobel Prize."

"How?" Asks the puzzled Hampshire man.

"Well," says the farmer, "I heard they give the prize to people who are outstanding in their field."

A police officer was patrolling the lanes outside Basingstoke one night, when he noticed a car swerving all over the road. Quickly, he turned on his lights and siren and pulled the driver over. "Sir, do you know you're all over the road? Please step out of the car."

When the man got out of the car, the policeman told him to walk in a straight line.

"I'd be happy to, offisher," said the drunk, "If you can just get the line to stop moving about."

A rabbit went to the fortune-teller.

"What do you see in my future?" asked the rabbit.

"Very soon," replied the fortune-teller, "you will meet a pretty young girl who will want to know everything about you, inside and out."

"That's great!" said the rabbit, hopping up and down. "But when will I meet her?" "Next week," said the fortune-teller, "in biology class."

At a cricket match in Purbrook, a fast bowler sent one down and it just clipped the bail. As nobody yelled "Ow's att", the batsman picked up the bail and replaced it. He looked at the umpire and said, "Windy today isn't it?"

"Yes," said the umpire, "Mind it doesn't blow your cap off when you're walking back to the pavilion."

What do you call the two people that always have to embarrass you the most in front of all your friends? Mum and Dad.

A policeman stops a drunk wandering the streets of Portsmouth at four in the morning and says, "Can you explain why you are out at this hour, sir?"

The drunk replies, "If I was able to explain myself, I would have been home with the wife ages ago."

A DEFRA Inspector goes to a small farm near Andover and knocks the door of the humble, tied cottage. A young boy opens the door and asks what business the man has on his parent's property.

"I've come to inspect the farm for compliance with EU regulations, my boy. Where's your father?"

"You can't speak to him, he's busy," says the surly child.

"I shall speak to him. He's had notice of my visit," the Inspector retorted firmly.

"Well, he's feeding the pigs at the moment," says the boy, "But you'll be able to tell me father easy enough - he's the one wearing a hat!"

One freezing cold December day, two blondes went for a walk in a wood near Warminster in search of the perfect Christmas tree. Finally, after five hours looking, one turns to the other and says crossly, "That's it, I've had enough. I'm chopping down the next fir tree we see, whether it's decorated or not!"

An elderly couple from Fleet are sitting at the dining table in their semi-detached house talking about making preparations for writing their wills. Bill says to his missus, Edna, "I've been thinking, my dear, if I go first to meet me maker I don't want you to be on your own for too long. In fact, I think you could do worse than marry Colin in the Chemists or Dave with the fruit stall in the market. They'd provide for you and look after you when I'm gone."

"That's very kind on you to think about me like that, Bill," replied Edna, "But I've already made my own arrangements!"

Miss Malaprop was telling a colleague about the wonderful evening she had had the night before at the ballet. She commented on the wonderful costumes, the fantastic orchestra and, most of all, on how graceful the dancers were, "They just slid across that stage like they were on casternets!"

A reporter from The Hampshire Chronicle was covering the local football league and went to see Liss Athetic F.C. versus Liphook United. One of the Liss players looked so old he went over to him and said, "You know you might be the oldest man playing in the league. How do you do it at your age?"

The man replied, "I drink six pints every night, smoke two

packets of fags a day, and eat tons of chips."

"Wow, that is incredible!" said the reporter, "How old did you say you were?"

"Twenty-two," said the player proudly.

An Alton couple, Enid and Sidney, are having matrimonial difficulties and seek the advice of a counsellor. The couple are shown into a room where the counsellor asks Enid what problems, in her opinion, she faces in her relationship with Sidney.

"Well," she starts, "he shows me no affection, I don't seem to be important to him anymore. We don't share the same interests and I don't think he loves me at all." Enid has tears in her eyes as the counsellor walks over to her, gives her a big hug and kisses her firmly on the lips.

Sidney looks on in passive disbelief. The counsellor turns to Sidney and says, "This is what Enid needs once a day for the next month. Can you see that she gets it?"

Sidney looks unsettled, "Well I can drop her off everyday other than Wednesdays when I play snooker and Sundays when I go fishing!"

A man from Bishops Waltham went into a hardware store and asked to buy a sink.

"Would you like one with a plug?" asked the assistant.

"Don't tell me they've gone electric now!" said the man.

Why is a clock like a depressed person? It's forever running itself down!

A man went to the doctor one day and said, "I've just been playing rugby for Eastleigh and when I got back, I found that when I touched my legs, my arms, my head, and everywhere else, it really hurt."

After a careful examination the doctor concluded, "you have a broken finger."

What do you get if you cross the Swindon Town with an OXO cube?

A laughing stock.

A woman got on a bus in Basingstoke but soon regretted it. The driver sped down the high street, zigzagging across the lanes, breaking nearly every rule of the road. Unable to take it any longer, the woman stepped forward, her voice shaking as she spoke. "You're a shocking driver! I am so afraid of sitting on your bus, I don't know what to do."

"Do what I do," said the bus driver. "Close your eyes!"

"Dad," says the little boy," Can I play football with the lads in the street?"

"No," says his dad, "They swear too much."

"But you play with them, Dad?"

"I swear already."

A labourer in Southampton, shouted up to his roofer mate on top of an old terraced house, saying, "Don't start climbing down this ladder, Bert."

"Why not?" Bert called back.

"Cos I moved it five minutes ago!" replied his mate.

A police officer arrived at the scene of a major pile up on the M27.

The officer runs over to the front car and asks the driver, "Are you seriously hurt?"

The driver turns to the officer and says, "How should I know? Do I look like a lawyer?"

There's a man in Chipping Sodbury who claims to have invented a game that's a bit like cricket; what he doesn't realise is Wiltshire County Cricket Club's been playing it for years.

A bloke walked up to the foreman of a road laying gang in Portsmouth and asked for a job. "I haven't got one for you today," said the foreman, looking up from his newspaper. "But if you walk half a mile down there, you'll find the gang and you can see if you like the work. I can put you on the list for tomorrow."

"That's great, mate," said the bloke as he wandered off down the road.

At the end of the shift, the man walked past the foreman and shouted, "Thanks, mate. See you in the morning."

The foreman looked up from his paper and called back, "You've enjoyed yourself then?"

"Yes, I have!" the bloke shouted, "But can I have a shovel or a pick to lean on like the rest of the gang tomorrow?"

Sam worked in a telephone marketing company in Havant. One day he walked into his boss's office and said, "I'll be honest with you, I know the economy isn't great, but I have three companies after me, and, with respect, I would like to ask for a pay rise."

After a few minutes of haggling, his manager finally agreed to a 5% pay rise, and Sam happily got up to leave.

"By the way," asked the boss as Sam went to the door, "Which three companies are after you?"

"The electric company, the water company, and the phone company," Sam replied.

A farmer was driving along a country road near the village of Chilbolton with a large load of fertiliser. A little boy, playing in front of his home, saw him and called out, "What do you have on your truck?"

"Fertiliser," the farmer replied.

"What are you going to do with it?" asked the little boy.

"Put it on strawberries," answered the farmer.

"You ought to live here," the little boy advised him. "We put sugar and cream on ours."

Wiltshire man: "I saw some cattle in a little village in Hampshire?"

Hampshire man: "Cowplain?"

Wiltshire man: "No, they had lovely eyes."

First man: "I picked up a rash when I was somewhere near Southampton."

Second man: "Itchen?"

First man: "I'll say it does!"

It was a quiet night in Aldershot and a man and his wife were fast asleep, when there was an unexpected knock on the door. The man looked at his alarm clock. It was half past three in the morning. "I'm not getting out of bed at this time," he thought and rolled over.

There was another louder knock.

"Aren't you going to answer that?" asked his wife irritably.

So the man dragged himself out of bed and went downstairs. He opened the door to find a strange man standing outside. It didn't take the homeowner long to realise the man was drunk.

"Hi there," slurred the stranger. "Can you give me a push?"

"No, I'm sorry I most certainly can't. It's half past three in the morning and I was in bed," said the man and he slammed the front door.

He went back up to bed and told his wife what happened.

"That wasn't very nice of you," she said. "Remember that night we broke down in the pouring rain on the way to pick the kids up from the babysitter, and you had to knock on that man's door to get us started again? What would have happened if he'd told us to get lost?"

"But the man who just knocked on our door was drunk," replied her husband.

"Well, we can at least help move his car somewhere safe and sort him out a taxi," said his wife. "He needs our help."

So the husband got out of bed again, got dressed, and went downstairs. He opened the door, but couldn't to see the stranger anywhere so he shouted, "Hey, do you still want a push?"

In answer, he heard a voice call out, "Yes please!"

So, still unable to see the stranger, he shouted, "Where are you?"

"I'm over here, mate," the stranger replied, "on your swing."

The president of the Winchester Vegetarian Society really couldn't control himself any more. He simply had to try some pork, just to see what it tasted like. So one day he told his members he was going away for a short break. He left town and headed to a restaurant in Alresford. He sat down, ordered a roasted pig, and waited impatiently for his treat. After only a few minutes, he heard someone call his name, and, to his horror, he saw one of his members walking towards him. At exactly the same moment, the waiter arrived at his table, with a huge platter, holding a whole roasted pig with an apple in its mouth. "Isn't this place something?" said the president, thinking quickly, "Look at the way they serve apples!"

Phil's nephew came to him with a problem. "I have my choice of two women," he said, with a worried frown, "A beautiful, penniless young girl whom I love dearly, and a rich widow who I don't really love."

"Follow your heart," Phil counselled, "marry the girl you love."

"Very well, Uncle Phil," said the nephew, "That's sound advice. Thank you."

"You're welcome," replied Phil with a smile, "By the way, where does the widow live?"

At a Ringwood school, the maths teacher poses a question to little Josh, "If I give £500 to your dad on 12% interest per annum, what will I get back after two years."

"Nothing," says Josh.

"I am afraid you know nothing about maths, Josh," says the teacher crossly.

"I am afraid too, sir," replies Josh, "You know nothing about my father."

Did you hear about the magic tractor? It drove up the lane and turned into a field.

There was a fight in the Indian restaurant...the chef is in hospital in a korma!

One Sunday in St Mary's church, Bentley, the vicar opened his Bible and began to read the lesson. In a loud voice, he proclaimed, "Corinthians 7."

A keen Southampton fan, who had been dozing in the front pew, woke up with a start and shouted out, "Blimey! Who were they playing?"

A passenger in a taxi tapped the driver on the shoulder to ask him something.

The driver screamed, lost control of the cab, nearly hit a bus, drove up over the curb and stopped just inches from a large plate glass window.

For a few moments everything was silent in the cab, then the driver said, "Please, don't ever do that again. You scared the daylights out of me."

The passenger, who was also frightened, apologised and said he didn't realise that a tap on the shoulder could frighten him so much, to which the driver replied, "I'm sorry, it's really not your fault at all. Today is my first day driving a cab. I've been driving a hearse for the last twenty-five years."

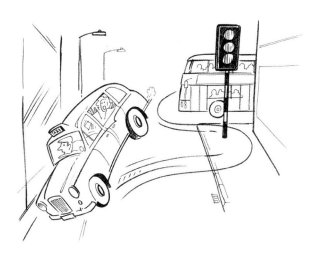

A high-rise building was going up in Southampton, and three steel erectors sat on a girder having their lunch.

"Oh, no, not cream cheese and walnut again," said Jim, the first one, "If I get the same again tomorrow, I'll jump off the girder."

Harry opened his packet. "Oh, no, not a Caesar salad with salami and lettuce on rye," he said. "If I get the same again tomorrow, I'll jump off too."

Orson, the third man, opened his lunch. "Oh, no, not another potato sandwich," he said. "If I get the same again tomorrow, I'll follow you two off the girder."

The next day, Jim got cream cheese and walnut. Without delay, he jumped. Harry saw he had Caesar salad with salami and

lettuce on rye and with a wild cry, he leapt too. Then the third man, Orson, opened his lunchbox. "Oh, no," he said. "Potato sandwiches." And he too jumped.

The foreman, who had overheard their conversation, reported what had happened, and the funerals were held together.

"If only I'd known," sobbed Jim's wife.

"If only he'd said," wailed Harry's wife.

"I don't understand it at all," said Orson's wife. "He always got his own sandwiches ready."

Wiltshire man: "There's a place in the Isle of Wight that does some really nice milk…"

Hampshire man: "Cowes?"

Wiltshire man: "No, goat's I think."

First man: "I took my mother to the zoo near Winchester yesterday…"

Second man: "Marwell?"

First man: "Yes, she's fine, thank you."

A farmer from Warminster once visited a farmer based near Liphook. The visitor asked, "How big is your farm?" to which the Hampshire farmer replied, "Can you see those trees over there? That's the boundary of my farmland".

"Is that all?" said the Wiltshire farmer, "It takes me three days to drive to the boundary of my farm."

The Liphook man looked at him and said, "I had a car like that once."

The nervous young batsman playing for Sarisbury Athletic C.C. was having a very bad day. In a quiet moment in the game, he muttered to the one of his team mates, "Well, I suppose you've seen worse players."

There was no response...so he said it again, "I said 'I guess you've seen worse players.'"

His team mate looked at him and answered, "I heard you the first time. I was just trying to think..."

When the manager of Swindon Town started to tell the team about tactics, half the players thought he was talking about a new kind of peppermint.

At a pub in Whitchurch, a newcomer asked a local man, "Have you lived here all your life?"

The old man took a sip of his ale and, after a long pause, replied, "Don't know yet!"

I had a car accident with a Magician - he came out of nowhere.

Supporters, waiting to watch Portsmouth F.C. play Swindon Town, heard that the Swindon players were going to be delayed.

They saw a sign on the motorway that said "Clean Lavatories"... so they did.

A man rushed into Royal South Hants Hospital and asked a nurse for a cure for hiccups. Grabbing a cup of water, the nurse quickly splashed it into the man's face.

"What did you that for?" screamed the man, wiping his face.

"Well, you don't have the hiccups now, do you?" said the nurse.

"No," replied the man. "But my wife out in the car does."

Did you hear about the fight in the chip shop last week? Six fish got battered!

A busy career man, tired of his daily commute from Winchester to London, decided he was going to give up his job, buy some land, and become a chicken farmer. He was lucky enough to find a chicken farm for sale at Sutton Scotney so he bought it and moved in. It turned out that his next door neighbour was also a chicken farmer. The neighbour came for a visit one day and said, "Chicken farming isn't easy, you know. To help you get started, I'll give you a hundred chickens."

The former career man was delighted. Two weeks later the neighbour dropped by to see how things were going. The new farmer said, "Not too well, mate. All hundred chickens died."

The neighbour said, "Oh, I can't believe that. I've never had any trouble with my chickens. I'll give you a hundred more."

Another two weeks went by and the neighbour dropped in again. The new farmer said, "You're not going to believe this, but the second lot of chickens died too."

Astounded, the neighbour asked, "What went wrong?" The new farmer shook his head, "I really don't know. Do you think I could be planting them too deep or too close together?"

An Aldershot woman called Alison was still not married at thirty-five and she was getting really tired of going to family weddings especially because her old Aunt Maud always came over and said, "You're next!"

It made Alison so annoyed, she racked her brains to figure out how to get Aunt Maud to stop. Sadly, an old uncle died and there was a big family funeral. Alison spotted Aunt Maud in the crematorium, walked over, pointed at the coffin and said, with a big smile, "You're next!"

There were two fish in a tank, one says, "You man the guns, I'll drive."

Peter walked up to the sales lady in the clothing department of a well known shop in Southampton.

"I would like to buy my wife a pretty pair of tights," he said. "Something cute with love-hearts or flower patterns."

"Oh, that's so sweet," exclaimed the sales lady, "I'll bet she'll be really surprised." "I'll say," said Peter, "she's expecting a new diamond ring!"

A pupil at a school in Purbrook asked his teacher, "Are 'trousers' singular or plural?"

The teacher replied, "They're singular on top and plural on the bottom."

One day at Queen Alexandra's Hospital in Portsmouth, a group of primary school children were being given a tour. A nurse showed them the x-ray machines and asked them if they had ever had broke a bone.

One little boy raised his hand, "I did!"

"Did it hurt?" the nurse asked.

"No!" he replied.

"Wow, you must be a very brave boy!" said the nurse. "What did you break?"

"My sister's arm!"

A man and his wife walked past a swanky new restaurant in Andover. "Did you smell that food?" the woman asked. "Wonderful!"

Being the kind-hearted, generous man that he was, her husband thought,

"What the heck, I'll treat her!"

So they walked past it a second time.

For a minute Swindon Town were in with a chance- then the game started.

Many years ago there was a dispute between two villages, one in Hampshire and the other in Wiltshire. One day the villagers heard the cry, "One man from Hampshire is stronger than one hundred Wiltshire men."

The villagers in Wiltshire were furious and immediately sent their hundred strongest men to engage with the enemy. They listened, horrified by the screams and shouts. After hours of fighting, all was quiet but none of the men returned.

Later on, the same voice shouted out, "Is that the best you can do?"

This fired up the people from Wiltshire and they rallied round, getting a thousand men to do battle. After days of the most frightful blood-curdling sounds, one man emerged from the battlefield, barely able to speak, but with his last breath he managed to murmur, "It's a trap, there's two of them!"

Did you hear about the truck driver from Gosport who was seen desperately chiselling away at the brickwork after his lorry became stuck at the entrance to a tunnel?

"Why don't you let some air out of your tyres?" asked a helpful passer-by.

"No, mate," replied the driver, "It's the roof that won't go under, not the wheels."

Did you hear about the last wish of the henpecked husband of a house-proud wife?

He asked to have his ashes scattered on the carpet.

Pete and Larry hadn't seen each other in many years. They were having a long chat, telling each other all about their lives. Finally Pete invited Larry to visit him in his new flat in Havant. "I have a wife and three kids and I'd love to have you visit us."

"Great. Where do you live?"

"Here's the address. There's plenty of parking behind the flat. Park and come around to the front door, kick it open with your foot, go to the lift and press the button with your left elbow, then enter! When you reach the sixth floor, go down the hall until you see my name on the door. Then press the doorbell with your right elbow and I'll let you in."

"Great. But tell me…what is all this business of kicking the front door open, then pressing elevator buttons with my right, then my left elbow?"

Pete answered, "Surely you're not coming empty-handed?"

"You're looking glum," the captain of Crown Taverner's remarked to one of his players.

"Yes, the doctor says I can't play cricket,' said the downcast man.

"Really?" replied the captain, "didn't know he'd ever seen you play?"

One day a Wiltshire boy was in the back garden shouting,

"Mum, why is my Swindon Town top lying on the grass?"

His Mum looked out the window and shouted,

"The thieving gits stole my pegs!"

A man from Devizes bought two horses, but soon realised that he couldn't tell them apart. So he asked the farmer, who lived next door, what he should do. The farmer suggested measuring them. The man came back triumphantly and said, "The white horse is two inches taller than the black horse!"

Have you heard about the latest machine in the arcade in Basingstoke town centre?

You put ten pence in and ask it any question and it gives you a true answer.

One visitor from Swindon tried it last week.

He asked the machine "Where is my father?" The machine replied:

"Your father is fishing in Trowbridge."

"Well," he thought, "That's daft for a start because my father is dead."

Next he asked, "Where is my mother's husband?"

The reply came back, "Your mother's husband is buried in Old Sarem, but your father is still fishing in Trowbridge."

At an antiques auction in Winchester, a wealthy American announced that he had lost his wallet containing £5,000, and he would give a reward of £50 to the person who found it.

From the back of the hall a local man shouted, "I'll give £100!"